Level
2

The Nature Kid's Guide to
OWLS

RENATA MARIE

LP Media Inc. Publishing
Text copyright © 2023 by LP Media Inc.
All rights reserved.

For information address LP Media Inc. Publishing,
3178 253rd Ave. NW, Isanti, MN 55040
www.lpmedia.org

Publication Data

Owls
The Nature Kid's Guide to Owls — First edition.

Summary: "Learn all about Owls, the Nature Kid Way"
— Provided by publisher.

ISBN: 978-1-954288-68-3

[1. Owls – Non-Fiction] I. Title.

Title: The Nature Kid's Guide to Owls

CONTENTS

SILENT
HUNTERS

Hoot! **A Eurasian eagle-owl flies through the skies.**

Owls fly over forests. They sail across deserts and dive through mountains. They dig homes under grasslands and hide in the snow.

Owls live all over the world. Their heads turn. Their eyes watch. They are the silent hunters of the night.

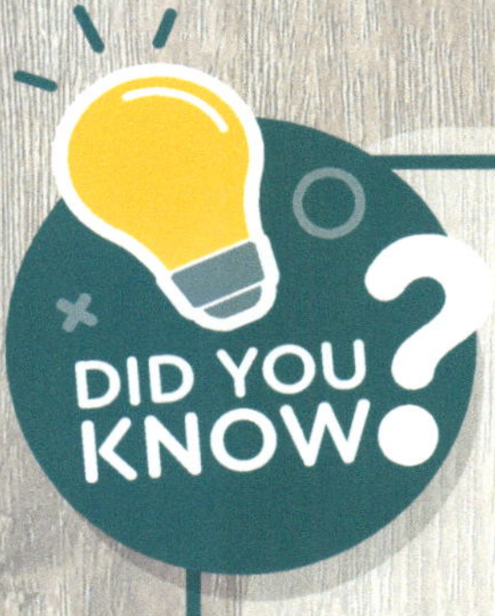

There are over 200 types of owls in the world. Nineteen types live in North America. Antarctica is the only place owls do not live.

BIG AND SMALL

A Great Grey owl lifts his wings. He is getting ready to fly.

Some owls are big. And some are small. Great Grey owls are the biggest owls in North America. Their wings reach five feet (1.5 meters). They weigh over four pounds (1.8 kilograms).

Elf owls are the smallest owls in the world. They live in North America. Their wings reach ten inches (25 centimeters). They only weigh 1.5 ounces (43 grams).

Blakiston's fish owls are the largest owls in the world. Their wings reach over six feet (1.8 m).

BIRDS OF PREY

A Long-eared owl sits in a tree. Her big eyes stare into the night.

Owls are birds of **prey**. They have big eyes. They can turn their heads 270 degrees.

They have sharp hearing. Their feathers help owls **camouflage** themselves. They help them look like trees and snow. Their wings are silent. Their talons are sharp. So are their beaks.

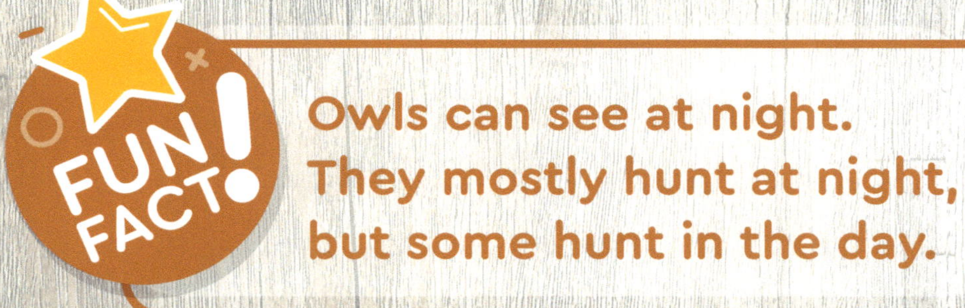

BONES AND FEATHERS

A Snowy owl sees a mouse. He dives for his next feast.

Owls are **carnivores**. **They eat meat.** They hunt mice, voles, rats, rabbits, skunks, squirrels, and frogs. They eat insects, snakes, birds, lizards, bats, and fish.

Bigger owls can hunt larger prey. They hunt weasels, foxes, and young deer.

Owls throw up what they cannot digest. They spit out balls of bones, fur, and feathers.

HIDDEN
OWLS
12

A tree branch turns its head. It is a Scops owl.

Owls use camouflage to hide from other animals. Owls that live in the forest stand tall. They hold their wings close. Their gray and brown feathers look like tree bark.

Snowy owls live in the Arctic. Their white feathers help them hide in the snow.

Burrowing owls have brown and white feathers. They match the ground they dig in.

SPOTTED
Badger
Bobcat
Fox
Hawk
Raccoon
14

A Great Horned owl eyes an eagle. He is ready to fight.

Owls hide from predators. Larger owls are rarely hunted. Smaller owls have more predators.

Owls have to watch out for eagles, hawks, foxes, wolves, snakes, badgers, coyotes, bobcats, raccoons, and ringtails. They even have to watch out for other owls.

When spotted, owls fight back. They open their wings. They fluff their feathers. They hiss. They snap their beaks. They use their sharp talons.

DID YOU KNOW?

Elf owls play dead if they are caught. When a predator loosens its hold, the owl flies away.

SHARP
EARS

***Scratch.* A Barred owl turns her head. She hears a mouse.**

Owls also hide from their prey. They sit in trees and listen.

Owls have sharp hearing. One ear is higher than the other. This helps them pinpoint where an animal is. They can hear prey ten miles (16 kilometers) away. They can even hear prey hidden under the snow.

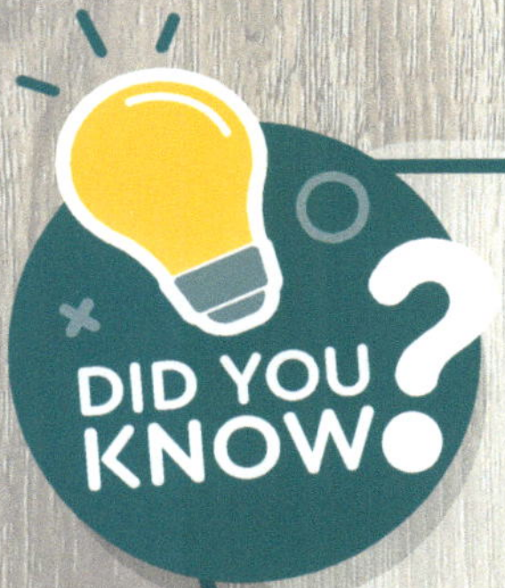

An owl's round face helps sound go to its ears.

QUIET FLIERS

A Barn owl flies silently into the night.

Owls fly silently. Owls have large wings. They rarely flap. They sail low to the ground.

Their feathers have comb-like edges. They break up the air. Their wings do not make a sound. Animals do not hear owls coming until it is too late.

Owls can fly up to 40 miles (64 km) per hour.

WHAT A
CATCH!
20

Talons rip through the snow. A mouse is lifted into the sky.

Owls attack prey with their talons. They fly close to their prey. They stretch their talons forward. They catch their prey.

Owls use their sharp beaks to tear their food. Or they swallow it whole.

FUN FACT!

Some owls keep food in hiding spots. They hide it in tree holes. They hide it behind grass and rocks.

HOOT IN A HOLE

An owl pops out of a hole. She runs across the ground.

Most owls fly over their prey. **Burrowing owls also hunt on the ground.** Their legs are long. They walk across the open land. They run and hop.

They hunt grasshoppers, beetles, and other bugs. They hunt snakes and frogs. They catch mice and small birds in their talons.

After eating, they rest in their nests.

Burrowing owls nest in holes under the ground.

WARM
IN A NEST

A Spotted Eagle-owl lies in a nest. She warms her eggs.

Owls sleep in nests. They use nests built by other birds. They nest in holes in trees and cliffs. They nest in barns and buildings.

Burrowing owls use holes dug by prairie dogs, badgers, skunks, and other digging animals. Sometimes they dig their own holes.

Snowy owls scrape shallow nests in the ground.

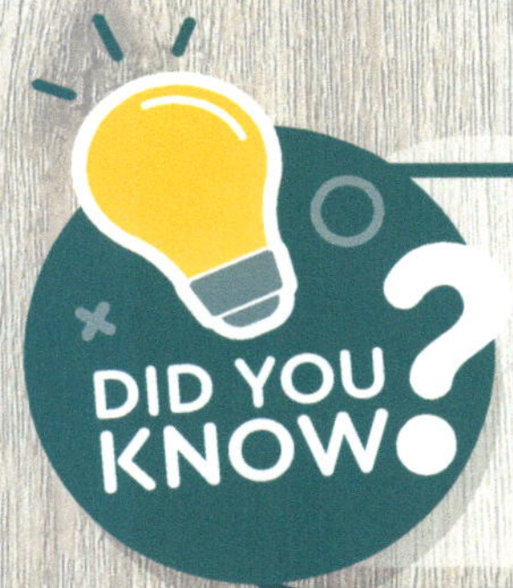

Catching lots of prey allows an owl to lay more eggs.

LITTLE OWLS

Eyes peek out from fluffy faces. It's a nest of Spotted owlets.

Mother owls can lay up to 13 eggs. They lie on them to keep them warm. They keep them safe from predators.

In about one month, the eggs crack open. **Baby owls are called owlets.** Their eyes are closed. They have fluffy feathers. Soon, their eyes will open.

Owls tear prey into tiny pieces. They feed their hungry owlets.

Male owls hunt for females and owlets. They bring prey back to their nests.

TAKE
FLIGHT!

A Great horned owlet inches along a branch. He cannot fly. But he wants to try.

Before owlets can fly, they climb on branches. They flap their wings. They try to make short flights. **Soon, the owlets will take to the skies.**

Some owls fly across lands. Snowy owls nest in the Arctic. In the winter, they fly south. They go where there is prey.

Snowy owls sometimes fly as far south as Texas and Florida.

LOVE
BIRDS

A hoot travels through a forest.

In the fall, male and female owls call to each other. When they meet, the male shows off.

He does a dance in the sky. He gives the female owl prey as a gift. If she likes him, they will find a nest together for the winter and raise owlets. Most owls stay together for life.

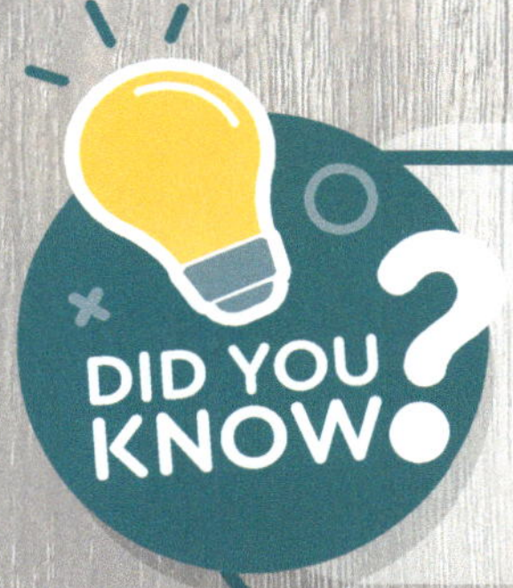

Paired owls rub their beaks on each other's heads. They clean each other's feathers.

FALLING FORESTS

Trees fall. Ice melts. Owls are in danger.

Owls have to watch out for more than predators. **Some types of owls are at risk of dying out.**

The earth is warming. Their homes are becoming smaller. There is less prey. People are hunting owls. They try to catch them.

KIDS CAN HELP THE EARTH

Close doors to keep the heat in

Plant a tree

Grow your own vegetables and fruits

34

A Barn owl sails through the sky. She looks for a safe place to nest.

As the Earth warms, the weather changes. **Owls are facing harmful weather.** Snow and ice melt. Holes flood. Forests dry up. They burn.

Owls are losing their homes. They are losing their prey, and not just because of the weather.

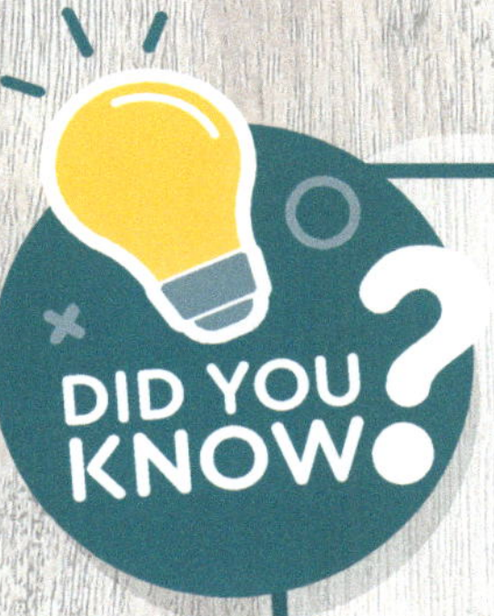

Sometimes wildfires are started by humans. Do not light fires when it is dry, hot, and windy. Keep an eye on campfires. Keep candles away from anything that can burn.

FLYING FREE

A Boreal owl rests in a box. She and her owlets are safe.

People are trying to help owls. They make nesting sites safe. They help plant new forests. They build nest boxes for owls. They stop using poisons to kill bugs and mice that owls might eat.

People hope that one day, owls will fly free once more.

Sometimes owls hit windows. But people can help them. They can put stickers on the outside of windows. Then owls can see the windows and stay away.

GLOSSARY

camouflage
something that helps
an animal hide
page 9

carnivores
animals that eat meat
page 11

predators
animals that hunt other
animals
page 15

prey
animals that are hunted by
other animals
page 9

MORE AMAZING ANIMAL BOOKS
from Nature Kids Publishing!

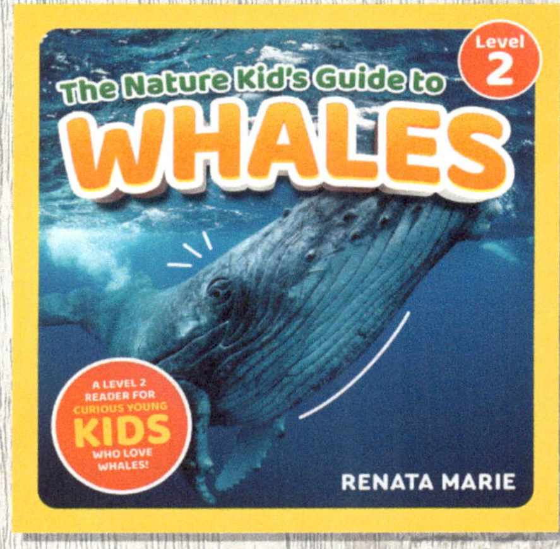

Visit NatureKidsPublishing.com
to Learn More!